ENGLAND
IN THE WEST INDIES

A NEGLECTED AND
DEGENERATING EMPIRE

By George Reginald Margetson

COPYRIGHT 1906
BY GEORGE REGINALD MARGETSON
CAMBRIDGE, MASS.

In the interest of creating a more extensive selection of rare historical book reprints, we have chosen to reproduce this title even though it may possibly have occasional imperfections such as missing and blurred pages, missing text, poor pictures, markings, dark backgrounds and other reproduction issues beyond our control. Because this work is culturally important, we have made it available as a part of our commitment to protecting, preserving and promoting the world's literature. Thank you for your understanding.

"In all my wanderings through this world of care,
In all my griefs — and God has given my share —
I still had hopes, my latest hours to crown,
Amidst these humble bowers to lay me down;
To husband out life's taper at the close,
And keep the flame from wasting by repose:
I still had hopes, for pride attends us still,
Amidst the swains to show my book-learn'd skill;
Around my fire a evening group to draw,
And tell of all I felt, and all I saw:
And, as a hare whom hounds and horns pursue,
Pants to the place from whence at first she flew,
I still had hopes, my long vexations past,
Here to return — and die at home at last."

— "The Deserted Village," *Goldsmith.*

ENGLAND IN THE WEST INDIES

A NEGLECTED AND DEGENERATING EMPIRE

Old England, dearest motherland beloved!
Thy right to be unerring time has proved;
To guide, to govern, and to legislate,
To train thy sons thy laws to instaurate.

Thou art a power of monarchical birth,
That typifies God's kingdom here on earth,
So men may learn Jehovah's praise to sing,
And spread the truth of the immortal King.

Though skeptics may protest thy designation,
And eke denounce thy sceptred coronation,
Yet fate thus formed thee at its rude command,
And time has reared thee with its fertile hand.

From yonder sacred nook, whence sprung thy birth,
Far to the nethermost shores of all the earth
Stupendous piles, romantic ruins lay;
In vain they fell to check thy giant sway,

ENGLAND IN THE WEST INDIES

When Wellington, Nelson, Roberts — kings of war —
Forth their volcanic chivalry did pour;
While bellowing "Britons never shall be slaves,"
Pillaged and swept the hostile plains and waves.

All tongues and tribes have felt thy goodly might,
Which thou dost spend to spread the gospel light;
Thy mighty hand has vanquished piracy
And stopped the onward march of slavery.

England! as I descry each noble trait,
My duty shall with conscience it relate;
And still will I lay bare to thee thy faults,
E'en though I spy them cloaked in private vaults.

And all the more when that such faults affect
Thyself, whom 't is thine office to protect;
And surely he is not an honest friend
Who doth thy goodly parts alone commend.

For we should know precisely what we are,
To judge if such another's rights doth mar;
And we should know likewise what not are we,
If we would realize what we hope to be.

ENGLAND IN THE WEST INDIES

So let our friends in all be plain and true,
Their knowledge can our actions well construe;
For 'tis our friends, our own, when urged by love,
Whose wisdom only can our wrongs reprove.

England! thy name is ever dear to me,
The birthplace of my father's family,
The rampart of the noble, brave and free,
The refuge for all tribes in slavery.

St. Kitts, my birthplace, 'fore thine eyes doth rust,
Yet still I love thee, shall and ever must;
Yet would I tune my lyre thy good to sing,
Until no more I'm ruled by earthly king.

To tell my deepest love I must refrain,
For words are weak and efforts are in vain;
Nor can I ever hope in deed to show,
For all that man can do the world doth know.

And though I'm forced in other lands to dwell,
Yet naught on earth can ever break the spell
That binds me to my own dear native land,
Where first I felt a mother's kindly hand.

ENGLAND IN THE WEST INDIES

And as fate drives me further from that clime,
I'll string my harp her praises fair to chime;
And when on foreign shores no more I roam,
I'll turn me thence to dwell at my dear home.

For when this heart time-worn shall cease to beat,
And dust to dust and soul to soul shall meet;
When this same self returns to God in Grace,
My native land shall be my resting place.

For by those orbs her bounteous gift bestows,
Where towering Misery's sulphurous grandeur flows;
By those dear charms my memory still retains,
For them I'll bless her with my last remains.

A mother there have I near bent with years,
A father lies entombed long bathed in tears,
Whose stalwart sons all graced by foreign skies,
Enjoy the comfort which their own denies.

Companions of my youth, and kindred dear,
I never more can hope to meet them there,
For destitution sits o'er all the plain,
Driving her sons to wander o'er the main.

ENGLAND IN THE WEST INDIES

England! dost thou still claim those Caribbean Isles,
Where frowns Mt. Blake and dear Mt. Misery smiles,
Where Souffrière doth her fiery glories fling,
And crags and peaks with Nature's anthems ring?

Within those depths the mad volcano howls,
Where Pelee like a thousand monsters growls,
Where all the elements combine to tell
Of smiling Paradise or frowning Hell.

Where spring to nature lends a healing turn
When scorching summer-fires blaze and burn;
Where autumn flings her fortune o'er the land,
And winter mars it not with frosty hand.

Where boundless groves and wreathing orchards grow,
And healing streams and sparkling waters flow;
Upon whose sun-kissed hills and fertile plains
Fair nature in her sovereign verdure reigns.

Where gay wild-blossoms shed their fragrance sweet,
Beneath whose eaves the constant lovers meet;
Where flowerets all with Eden's splendour bloom,
To cheer the marriage and to mourn the tomb.

ENGLAND IN THE WEST INDIES

The moon, the stars, those wondrous orbs of light,
Transmit their rays and make glad day of night,
From heaven to earth in cheering beams look down,
And guide the traveller to his native town.

The soothing zephyr with its odorous wealth
Imparts a soul-balm to the broken health;
The prophet ground-dove with its warbling breath
Exhales its signal-song of coming death.

Then all at once there grows a dismal change,—
A rainbow spans the sky, all wild and strange,
Each roaming bird in haste now seeks its nest,
The storm-clouds marshal them from east and west.

The swelling sea takes on a snowy tinge—
A vast blue sheet decked with embroidered fringe—
While thick o'er all the storm its mantle flings,
And all the trees and houses flap their wings.

The fiery lightnings flash, the thunders roar,
And clouds in hissing showers their vengeance pour,
While choking gales or fierce tornadoes blow,
And torrents dark to main from mountain flow.

ENGLAND IN THE WEST INDIES

The invading sea its angry breast doth heave,
Whose furious waves their distant moorings leave;
While on the billows in the engulfing tide
Heroic barques like fearless monsters ride.

The deafening thunders leap o'er mountain peaks,
While God to man through tropic elements speaks
His mighty power and his wondrous love,
That bid the skeptic soul its doubts remove.

And as the increasing storm more fiercely howls,
The houseless insects, animals and fowls,
All in confusion flee from place to place
To find some calmer spot to hide their face.

The waters gush, the earth with terror quakes,
The god of havoc now himself awakes,
From Misery's heights directs his thundering host,
The heavens burst and all in gloom is lost.

See now the awe-struck husband, child and spouse,
Who, seeking shelter, rush from house to house;
While ghastly ruins strewn in every path
Bespeak the havoc of the tempest's wrath.

ENGLAND IN THE WEST INDIES

Great God, wilt Thou the elements exhaust?
Could nature's womb replace the dreadful cost?
The kneeling pine in mournful robe is clad,
The palm tree weeps and all is pale and sad.

The man, his wife and child, now take their knees,
Sweet Grace! the howling dog for mercy pleas,
The chattering stones all call upon their god,
Indeed the very ghost now seeks the sod.

But ah! as Heaven smiles and lifts the gloom,
All nature with redoubled life doth bloom;
Thus as the different seasons fall and rise,
They lend alternate hell and paradise.

Here men and dames of noble souls abound!
Here freedom's bell and friendship's harp resound!
Here Nelson once thy most revered, adored,
His heart in love to female virtue bowed!

What nature to mankind elsewhere denies,
In healing spells her blessing here supplies;
Here like a dream my youth's life-stream did run,
Nursed by her fertile dews and smiling sun.

ENGLAND IN THE WEST INDIES

Montserrat, Dominica, shrine-like island-springs,
Wherein thine ill-fledged creatures lave their wings,
Above whose meadowy fields glad warblers soar,
Within whose groves no ravenous echoes roar.

Barbadoes, nature's blessed and beauteous plain,
Fair link that joins thy boasted empire chain;
Antigua eke now wearing thy disdain,
Have fed thy councils with their mellow brain.

St. Lucia, Mistress of the Antilles,
Thy great Gilbraltar of the West Indies,
And Trinidad, strong in its asphalt lakes,
On them, on them Britannia's death-swell breaks.

Here naught save wild uncultivated fruit
In gorgeous glow of varied colours shoot;
These are the gifts that nature now bestows
To heal the life-wound of the tyrant's blows.

But for these needs which Heaven alone supplies,
No remnant being would breathe beneath these skies;
For when the dreadful scourge his power expands,
He makes a funeral of his captive bands.

ENGLAND IN THE WEST INDIES

Plantations where sweet canes did tempt the taste
Are left to wither as a barren waste;
The scorching power of time's terrific blast
Hath made a fertile plain a desert vast.

Sayst thou, Great Britain, that thou claimst them still,
And soon wilt shake them from their time-wrought ill?
Wilt shed in all their parts thy Christian deed,
Thy sons to heaven from earth-born hell to lead?

Wilt save the institution and the school,
And break the death lock of the tyrant's rule?
Wilt spread the bounty of thy generous hand,
And rear them once more to a healthful stand?

At fair Jamaica, thy dear island pearl,
Upon whose heights the winds thy colours curl,
See how thy priceless gems to ruins go!
Hark to thy sons and daughters' wails of woe!

See there appalled thy subject human scrag,
Unclothed, half-starved, yet loves, defends the flag!
Peer forth the window of thy soul, descry
Wherefore such destitution jeers the eye!

ENGLAND IN THE WEST INDIES

Now turn thee where that starry ensign waves,
Lo, how yon shores her maiden virtue laves!
See how her hand the despot's deed repairs,
And learn how thus her ceaseless bounty rears!

Hie thee to Cuba, once in hell-born gloom!
Greet Eden fair where heaven-born splendours bloom!
See her where war and famine once held sway!
Hail her where peace and plenty reign today!

As the good mother for her child provides,
And counsels it in love, in wisdom chides,
To face the wrath of time's contemptuous wave,
So should a nation for its subjects brave.

For 'tis the well-nursed branches of a tree,
Reared as a child upon its mother's knee
To vigorous health, a well-developed form,
That shield the mother trunk from wind and storm.

Therefore the mother who could not protect
Her child, or train it in each good respect,
Had better yield it to a guardian friend,
Who would instruct aright to noble end.

ENGLAND IN THE WEST INDIES

And then if she refuses to submit
Her tender issue unto one more fit
To wield the duty of a mother dear,
'Twould be most proper that she cease to bear.

England! hast thou forever turned thy neck
Against thy stricken child, whose strength did deck
Thy royal crown with fortune's choicest flowers,
That placed thee foremost in the ranks of powers?

Wilt thou not stoop to hear thy subject speak?
Canst thou not recognize its pallid cheek?
It is thine own, thy long-forsaken child,
Thy negligence its beauty hath defiled!

Wilt thou not hearken to its sad appeal?
Wilt thou not strive its wounded parts to heal?
Or wilt thou not some moral aid impart,
To soothe the sorrows of its care-worn heart?

How long wilt thou withhold a due return?
How long wilt thou thy subject justice spurn?
How long wilt thou a guardian's care pretend?
How long wilt thou refrain thy faults to mend?

ENGLAND IN THE WEST INDIES

When shall the lad his mother's face behold?
When shall the mother's breast its griefs unfold?
When, when shall she reclasp her wandering boy,
O when wilt thou repair their broken joy?

When shall the roaming lover claim his choice?
When shall the faithful maiden's heart rejoice?
How soon shall they fulfill their solemn vow?
What time shall they before the altar bow?

When shall the husband to his wife return?
When shall their love-flames cease in vain to burn?
When shall the father bless his children dear?
When shall he lead his house again in prayer?

When shall thy sons their kindred soil regain,
And ease their weary bones from toil and pain?
When shall their griefs and groanings see their end?
England! when will thy stiff-necked conscience bend?

Long, long our sufferings at thy feet have lain,
Still dost thou linger to relieve our pain;
Long hast thou housed and fed thy neighbors' well,
And let thine own dear children taste of hell.

ENGLAND IN THE WEST INDIES

It matters not though fertile be our lands,
E'en though we till with nimble hearts and hands;
Nor matters what the soil to yield be made,
We need must find a market for our trade.

Against us on all sides are tariff walls,
Whereon long beat in vain our commerce squalls;
Then, turning to thine own, our mother's fold,
We face the competition of the world.

Thy worthless commerce law by Gladstone made,
That may have flourished in a blind decade,
To thriftier thoughts and schemes must now give way:
The world is up and brighter far today.

Could free-trade passport ever yield a grain
To thee, existing as a split domain?
Would preferential tariff breed and shine
When all thy colonies with thee combine?

Would reciprocity reverse thy doom,
If such as thou produce not nor consume,
Within the limits of thy broad threshold,
In the commercial realm were bought and sold?

ENGLAND IN THE WEST INDIES

Or wouldst thou choose the tactics of a power
That seeks in others' fields her goods to shower,
And flood their various markets with her store,
Yet with protective tariff guards her door.

Would just retaliation save thy trade,
To pay to others what to thee were paid?
Or would a union of all commerce laws
Release thy babes from hell's infernal jaws?

When each succeeding effort naught would yield
Save thorns and briers as of sand-clad field,
Reform thy parliament, revise thy laws,
If thou wouldst justly work a nation's cause!

Methink that power is not worse by far
Which doth promote damned slavery or war,
And make the world a hell with butchery,
Than that which deals injustice to the free.

For when their fiendish business we compare,
One is a hungry lion, one a bear —
The daring lion boldly takes its prey,
The bear adopts a droll and subtle way.

ENGLAND IN THE WEST INDIES

Though one is harsh, one gentle in its way,
Both plunder flesh, for both are beasts of prey;
Though each pursues a different mode of strife,
There's but one common end, — both take thy life.

England! behold, reflect, repair thyself,
Thy wealth and virtue rot on yonder shelf;
Fast fades thy beauty and thy life abates,
Degeneration howls within thy gates.

"A chain is strong as is its weakest link,"
Then thou shouldst ponder o'er thy plight, methink!
Beshrew thy soul nor mock the welkin's elf!
If thou wouldst hold thy power, maintain thyself!

Great Britain! up! up with thy drooping knees!
Up from thy rest, thy long unbroken ease!
Beware! the warning billows onward roll,
Then upward, onward, reach the frontward goal.

England arise! quit now thy dismal sleep,
Prepare! time's foes around thy fortress creep;
Awake! or soon the nightmare seize its prey!
Thine empire tumbles and thy powers decay!

Printed by Libri Plureos GmbH in Hamburg, Germany